www.DyslexiaGames.com

Copyright © 2014 the Thinking Tree, LLC. All rights reserved.

Dyslexia Games
Friendly Copyright Notice:

ALL DYSLEXIA GAMES, WORKSHEETS, AND MATERIALS MAY <u>NOT</u> BE SHARED, COPIED, EMAILED, OR OTHERWISE DISTRIBUTED TO ANYONE OUTSIDE YOUR HOUSEHOLD OR IMMEDIATE FAMILY (SHARING IS STEALING).

Schools, Therapy Centers and Classroom Use: Please purchase a Teacher's License for reproduction of materials.

Please refer people interested in Dyslexia Games to our website to purchase their own copy of the materials.

The Thinking Tree LLC • 617 N Swope St. • Greenfield, IN 46140 • info@dyslexiagames.com • 317-622-8852

Think, Write & Draw

Use a smooth black pen or sharp pencil to complete each page. You may use a dictionary to help you find new words for some of these activities.

After every three pages is a "Be Creative Page" where you can spend some time doodling just for fun.

These games may seem simple, but are very helpful for training the right brain to engage in reading.

Can you write
5 words
and draw 1 picture
that starts with
this letter?

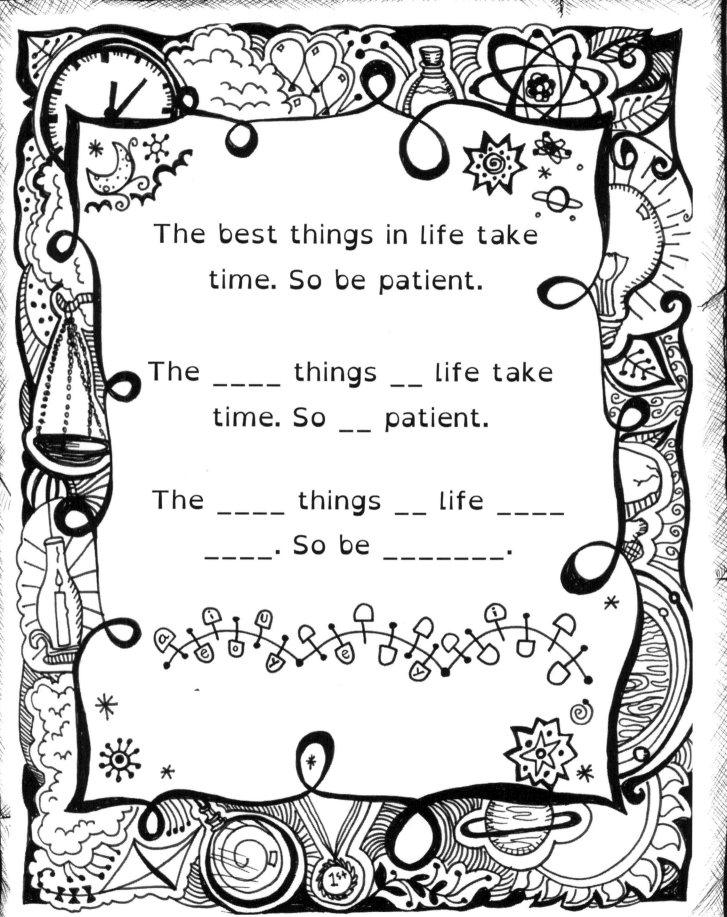

The best things in life take time. So be patient.

The ____ things __ life take time. So __ patient.

The ____ things __ life ____ ____. So be _____.

It's time to do whatever you want to with this page!

Always make ____ for the _____ that ___ love.

_____ make time ___ the people ____ you love.

Always ____ time for ___ _____ that you ____.

Can you write
5 words
and draw 1 picture
that starts with
this letter?

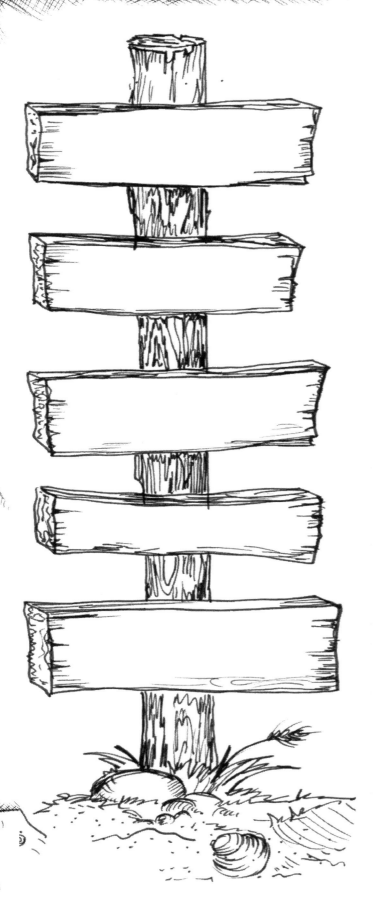

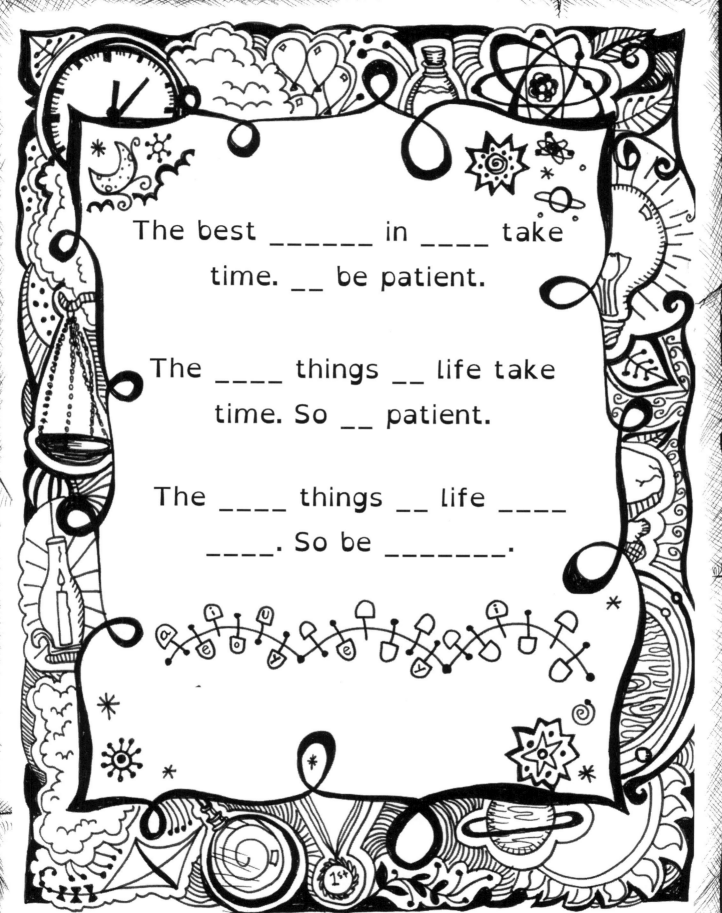

The best _____ in ____ take time. __ be patient.

The ____ things __ life take time. So __ patient.

The ____ things __ life ____ ____. So be _____.

It's time to do whatever you want to with this page!

Can you write
5 words
and draw 1 picture
that starts with
this letter?

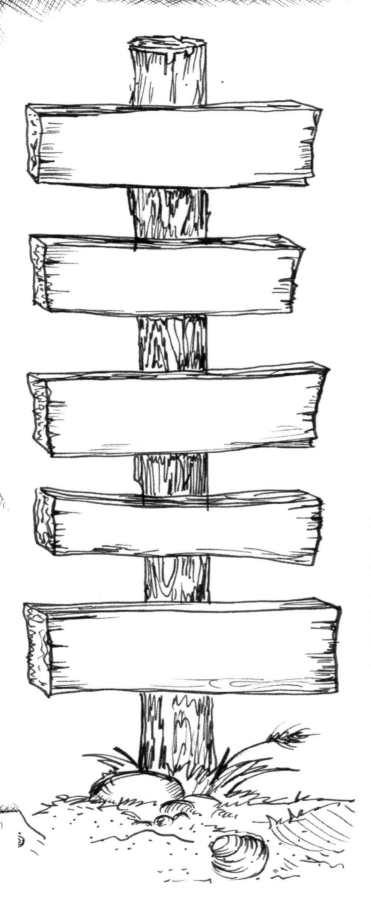

What __ you ____ to do with your ____? Start today!

____ do ___ want __do with ____ life? Start today!

____ do ___ want __ do ____ your ____? Start _____!

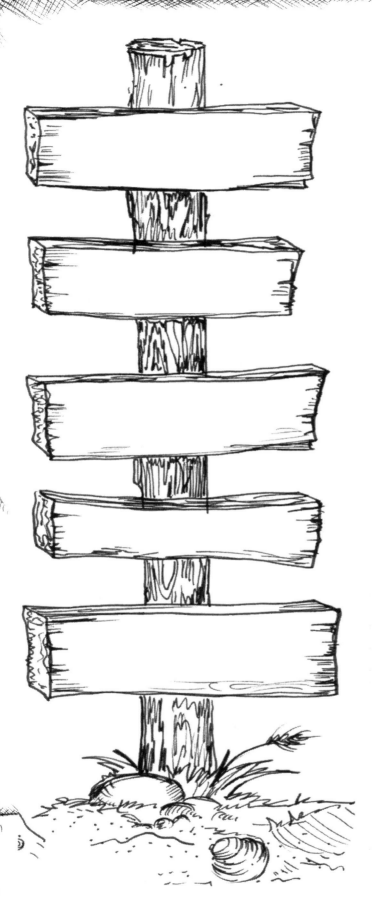

Can you write
5 words
and draw 1 picture
that starts with
this letter?

Live ___ the _____ that matter most and __ content.

____ for the things ____ _____ most ___ be content.

Live ___ the _____ that _____ ____ and __ content.

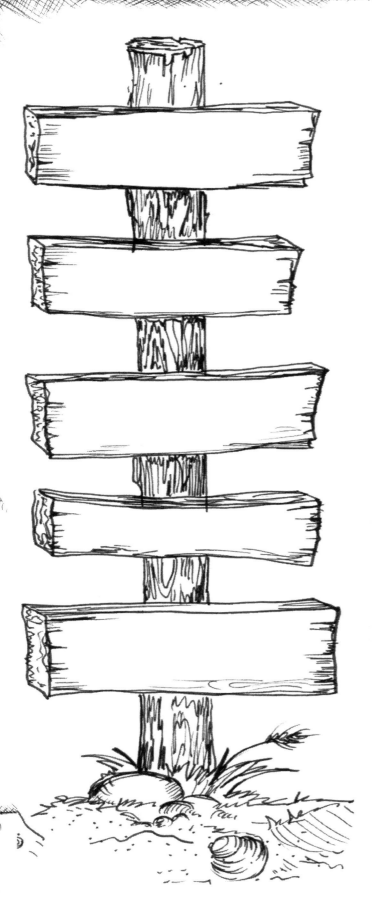

Can you write
5 words
and draw 1 picture
that starts with
this letter?

Be ___ kind of friend ____ you always wished you had.

Be the ____ of _____ that you _____ wished you had.

Be ___ kind __ friend ____ ___ always _____ you ___.

| ZNW | MLZ | ZN_ | M__ |

It's time to do whatever you want to with this page!

Can you write
5 words
and draw 1 picture
that starts with
this letter?

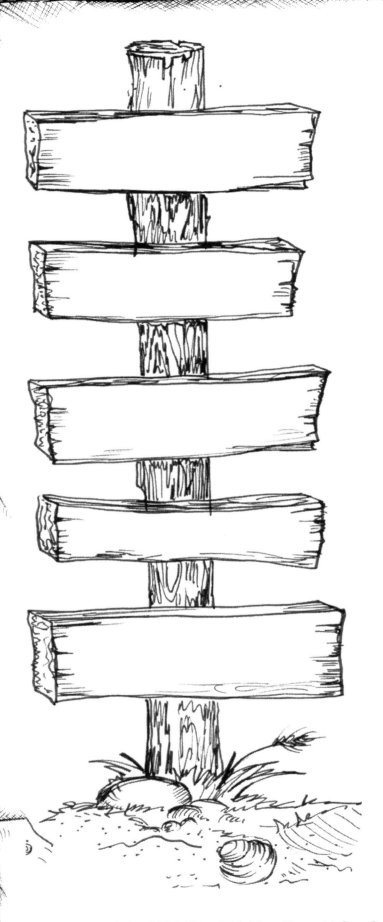

Can you write
5 words
and draw 1 picture
that starts with
this letter?

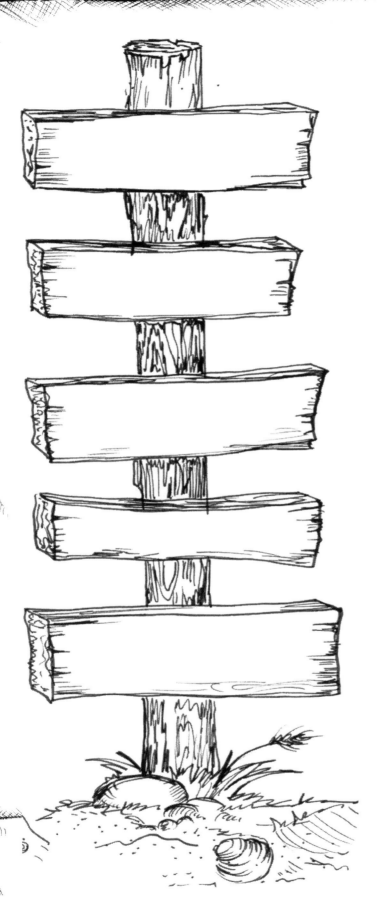

Always try to learn something new each day.

Always ___ to _____ something ___ each day.

_____ try __ learn _____ new ____ ___.

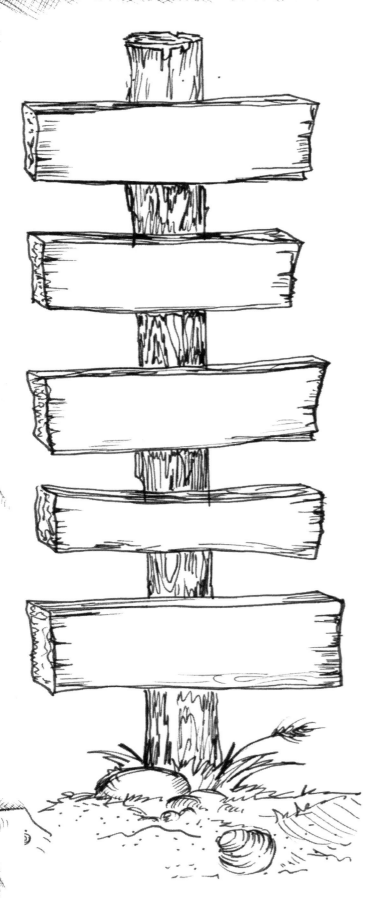

Can you write
5 words
and draw 1 picture
that starts with
this letter?

It's time to do whatever you want with this page!

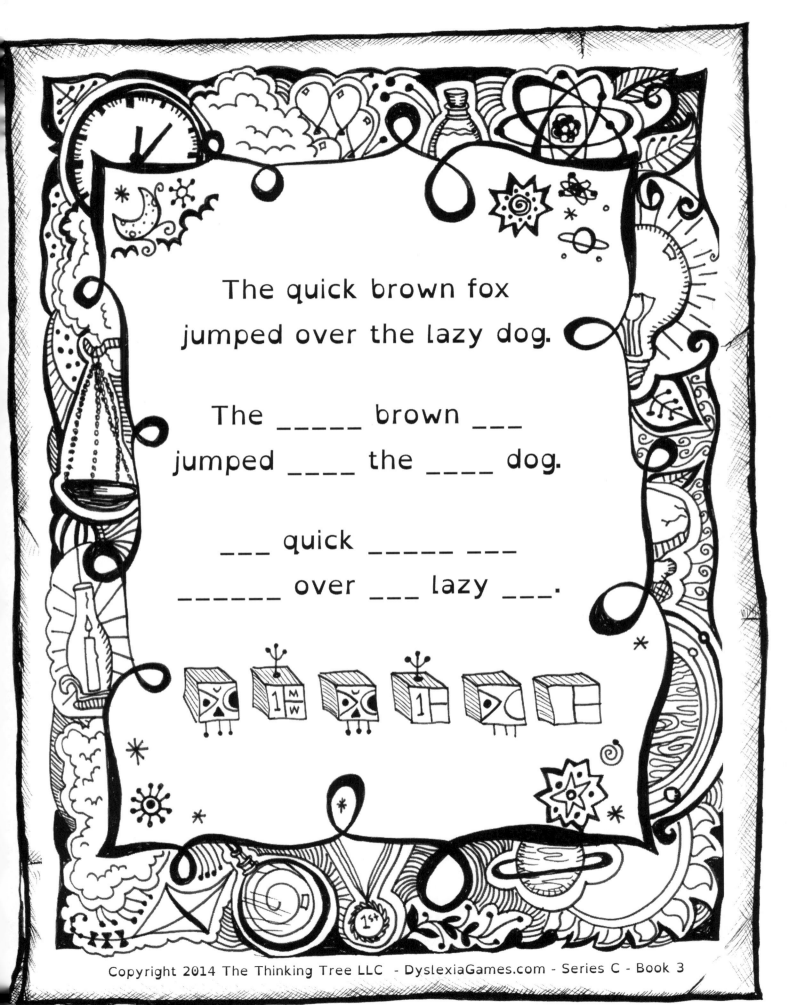

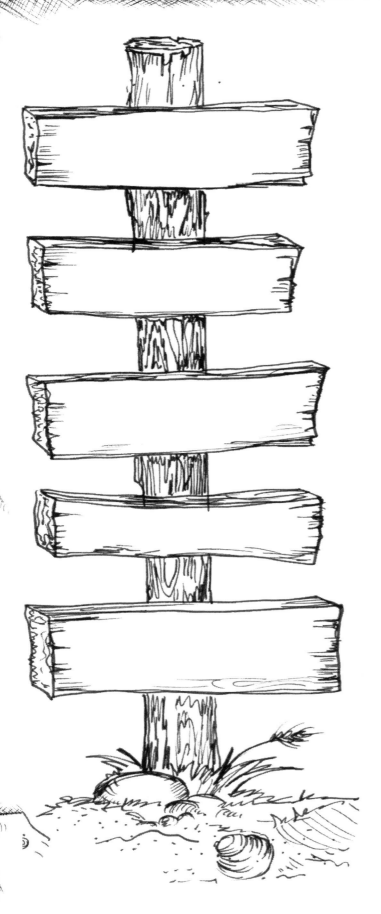

Can you write
5 words
and draw 1 picture
that starts with
this letter?

Can you write 5 words and draw 1 picture that starts with this letter?

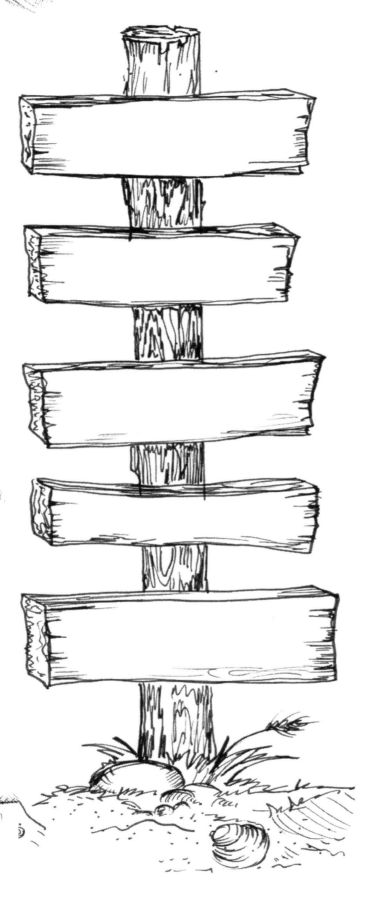

It's time to do whatever you want with this page!

Can you write
5 words
and draw 1 picture
that starts with
this letter?

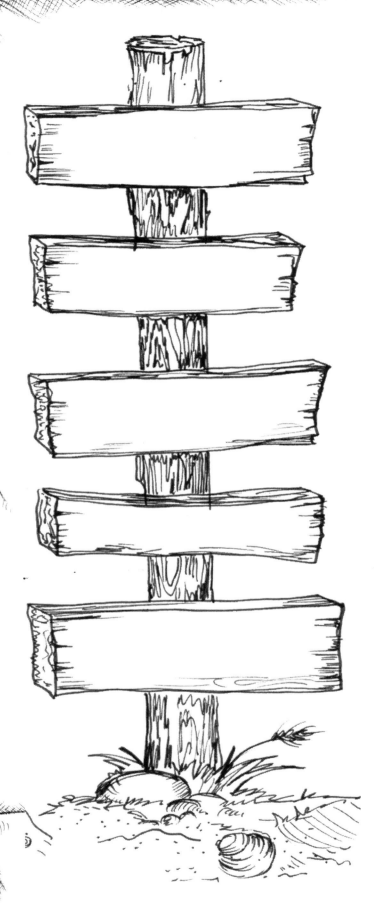

Can you write 5 words and draw 1 picture that starts with this letter?

It's time to do whatever you want with this page!